A WRITER'S NOTEBOOK

Other books about writing by
RALPH FLETCHER

Live Writing:
Breathing Life into Your Words

How Writers Work:
Finding a Process That Works for You

Poetry Matters:
Writing a Poem from the Inside Out

A WRITER'S NOTEBOOK

Unlocking the Writer Within You

Ralph Fletcher

📖 HarperTrophy®
An Imprint of HarperCollinsPublishers

CONTENTS

What Is a Writer's Notebook, Anyway?

Once, when I was a boy, a telephone repair truck pulled up in front of our house and two workers got out. They had come to lay a telephone cable. My brothers and sisters and I watched them work hard for almost three hours digging a long narrow ditch in our backyard. Finally, when it was starting to get dark, they left the ditch and went home, promising to return and finish the job the next morning.

Early the following morning I went outside and looked into that empty ditch. But it wasn't empty at all. I was amazed to find all sorts of small animals caught in there: four toads, two frogs, even a small box turtle. They must have wandered into the ditch, gotten stuck there, and been unable to climb back out. I let all the animals go. The two workers returned, finished laying the telephone cable, and covered up the ditch.

That got me thinking. The next day I decided to dig my own ditch. I dug it at the edge of the woods (I didn't think Dad would have appreciated seeing another ditch in our lawn) and made it about a foot wide, ten feet long, and eight inches deep. Next morning I hurried outside and discovered that—yes!—the same thing had happened. A number of small creatures had been caught in there.

A writer's notebook is like that ditch—an empty space you dig in your busy life, a space that will fill up with all sorts of fascinating little creatures. If you dig it, they will come. You'll be amazed by what you catch there.

Writing is what I do for my job. I've written books for adults and books for young readers. I've published a novel, several books of poetry, short stories, and books for teachers on how to teach writing. In this book I want to explore with you the most important tool I use: my writer's note-book. Keeping a writer's notebook is one of the best ways I know of living a writing kind of life.

What is a writer's notebook, anyway? Let's start by talking about what it's *not*. A writer's notebook is not a diary: "Today it is raining. We have a sub-stitute teacher named Miss Pampanella. She seems very nice. We are going to have gym right before lunch." It's not a reading journal in which your teacher tells you to summarize the main idea of a book, or write a letter to a character. A writer's notebook is different from any journal you've ever kept before.

Writers are pretty ordinary people. They have favorite songs, favorite movies, favorite TV shows. Writers have Evil Big Sisters (and, occasionally, sweet ones). They get good or not so good grades, take vacations, paint their houses . . .

Writers are like other people, except for at least one important difference. Other people have daily thoughts and feelings, notice this sky or that smell, but they don't do much about it. All those thoughts, feelings, sensations, and opinions pass through them like the air they breathe.

3

Not writers. Writers react. And writers need a place to record those reactions.

That's what a writer's notebook is for. It gives you a place to write down what makes you angry or sad or amazed, to write down what you noticed and don't want to forget, to record exactly what your grandmother whispered in your ear before she said good-bye for the last time.

A writer's notebook gives you a place to live like a writer, not just in school during writing time, but wherever you are, at any time of day.

A few years ago I was walking in Wheeling, Illinois, and I saw a rainbow so enormous it seemed to stretch from one horizon to the other. But there was something wrong with it—the topmost arch was missing. I came back to my hotel room, took out my notebook, and wrote:

The skies are so huge in the midwest! They just don't make skies like this back east. Today I saw a rainbow, beautiful and damaged, the top part washed away, gone. Never seen anything like it. Wonder what makes that happen. Had the winds swept away the highest clouds?

Months later I began writing a series of love poems. I reread my notebook and found that entry. The words—*a rainbow, beautiful,* and *damaged*—seemed to jump off the page. I used that phrase like a piece of flint to spark this sad poem I wrote:

First Flight

All the way home
I tried to forget
how your lip twitched
how your face flinched

I walked alone
under a huge rainbow
beautiful and damaged
upper arch worn away
just two broken pieces
dangling from the sky

What does a writer's notebook look like? There's really no right answer for this except that your writer's notebook should reflect your personality. Some writers prefer a pad small enough to stick in a back pocket. Others have beautiful notebooks with wildflowers on their covers, and others with plain brown covers. My wife's notebook has unlined pages because she likes to sketch in it, as well as write. My notebook is really supposed to be a business ledger, with lined, numbered pages. It has a hard cover and a very sturdy binding, which is good because I drag it with me wherever I go and it gets banged up a lot.

A notebook doesn't even have to be made from paper, really. Often I work on my "notebook computer" while I'm flying from one city to the next. But a notebook doesn't have to be expensive or fancy—a plain notebook from the stationery store will do just fine.

I hope you'll get yourself some kind of notebook and begin to write in it on a regular basis. In this book I suggest lots of ways you can use your writer's notebook to sift and collect important things from your life, stuff that may prove valuable in later writing. We'll also look at ways to reread your notebook and use what you have collected to generate your own "polished" writing.

In this book you'll find many examples from

my writer's notebook, the notebooks of published writers, and the notebooks of young writers like you. By sharing all these examples I hope to give you an idea of what's possible. Use the ideas you find here as springboards into what you can do with your own notebook.

Your notebook is uniquely yours, like your wallet or backpack. Only you can decide what to put in it. You probably won't use every idea you find in this book. If an idea doesn't grab you, just move on to the the next chapter. If you read an idea that appeals to you, try it out in your own notebook. Experiment!

When you come right down to it, a writer's notebook is nothing more than a blank book, but within those pages you've got a powerful tool for writing and living. In the pages that follow, we'll explore ways you can use your notebook so you can begin to live like a writer.

ONE

Unforgettable Stories

Does this ever happen to you? You stay up late on New Year's Eve and watch TV. Seems like everybody in the country has gone bananas, especially the crowd of people waiting for the ball to drop in Times Square in New York City. "Happy New Year's Eve!" people are shouting, jumping up and down as if they've just won the lottery. "Happy New Year!"

You say to yourself: What's the big deal?

You watch the opening ceremonies of the Olympic Games. Next day at school, people are talking about how beautiful it was, how colorful, how *awesome*. But you didn't find it the least bit beautiful, colorful, or awesome. You wonder: Is something wrong with me?

Then one summer day you happen to notice a small black ant dragging the body of another black ant along the sidewalk. Nobody else sees it, but for some reason this sight captures your interest; you squat down to take a closer look.

The ant is really working, straining to hoist a weight nearly equal to its own. A dozen questions crowd your mind. Is the ant carrying the body of a friend? A brother or child? If so, does it feel sad? Do ants have feelings? (Probably not.) Where is the ant taking the body? Is it going to feed the body to its babies? Are ants cannibalistic? You read that some ants actually build graveyards for the dead. Is the ant going to bury the body?

Later, up in your bedroom, you can't get it out of your head, the sight of that ant dragging the dead body along the sidewalk. It has stirred something inside you—you pick up your pen to write.

We live in a world where people are quick to tell us how to feel. TV commercials promise "an unforgettable vacation," a candy bar that will "have your taste buds popping wheelies on your tongue," a movie that will "make you want to stand up and cheer." But too often we end up feeling hollow instead.

When something truly touches you, it touches you on the inside, and you can't fake that. I watched on TV when the Boston Bruins held a special night to honor their hockey star, Bobby Orr. Just thirty years old, Orr was being forced by injuries to retire. I loved Orr. He was so unbelievably fast and skilled. You could take someone to a hockey game, someone who knew nothing about hockey, and you could say: "Watch number four— he's the best guy on the ice"—and you would always be right. That night when Bobby Orr appeared, the crowd erupted in an emotional six minute standing ovation that brought me to tears. My best friend, who couldn't care less about sports, watched and yawned.

People are different. What dazzles one person might bore the next. The question is: What moves you? As a writer, you need to be able to answer that question. And take note of it. Whenever I hear a story that stirs something inside me I take out my notebook and write.

October 18

Jerry Kelly told me something he heard from a young white teacher who works in an all-black school in East Harlem, New York. On Friday, the day of the Los Angeles riots, her students were afraid for her safety. After school they made a circle around her, walked her from the school to a safe place, and stayed there until she could get a taxi.

I look for stories, like this one, that inspire me. I look for what fascinates me or fills me with wonder. I look for stories that anger or disgust me, or make me laugh out loud.

Remember when that comet collided with Jupiter? This event, and the spectacular photographs of it, got a friend of mine all agitated.

"I was so shocked when that comet smacked into Jupiter," she said to me. "Didn't you feel sorry for poor old Jupiter?"

"Not really," I admitted. "For heaven's sake, Jupiter is a *planet*, not a human being! There's nothing living on it. It can't feel a thing."

She sniffed and stomped away. I didn't write

about this in my writer's notebook. But a few days later I heard on the radio a story about Vietnam, where so many American and Vietnamese soldiers lost their lives during the 1960s and 1970s. Some Vietnamese people believe the ghosts of the dead soldiers still wander the land at night. At night these people put out food so the ghosts will have something to eat. They put out Vietnamese food for the ghosts of the dead Vietnamese soldiers. But many American GIs died, too, so they put out American food for the ghosts of the dead American soldiers.

A story like this one simply refused to get out of my head; at night I found myself thinking about it before I fell asleep. In my writer's notebook I jotted down a few sentences about this strange hospitality to the ghosts of those dead soldiers.

At times you hear something on the news, or read something in a newspaper, that affects you strongly:

October 23

Been reading about all the flooding in the midwest. In one place there was a drive-through safari there. The zoo got flooded quickly and the zoo people didn't have enough advance warning to get the animals out. The animals were in cages nearly underwater so the zoo people had to go around and quickly shoot all the animals.

So horrible! I mean if people are going to capture wild, endangered animals and put them in our zoos, they better have a plan to keep them alive in an emergency like this.

Often the stories that tug hardest at our heart-strings are close to home:

- a woman you know who still puts roses on her husband's grave ten years after his death
- the courageous way your cat fought off a much larger cat who attacked it one night
- a local battle between people who want to preserve a nature sanctuary and those who want to build houses on that land
- a friend who lost his wallet with a hundred dollars cash in it; the wallet and money got returned by a young man who refused to accept a reward

The story could be something that happened to you:

Came home from school yesterday, Valentine's Day, and something really weird happened. Mom called from work asking me to go out and buy Dad a Valentine's card from her. I grumbled but said, all right, I'll do it. As soon as she hung up, Dad called. Would I do him a big favor and go out and buy Mom some chocolates from him for Valentine's Day?

What's wrong with those two?! Give me a break!

What moves you? What stories keep tumbling through your mind even when you try not to think about them? Jot them down in your writer's notebook. You might write the whole story, but you don't have to. You can also write down a key phrase (*L.A. riots—black kids making circle around white teacher*) as a mental place-holder to remind you until you have the chance to go back and write more about it.

Writers are people who have a keen nose for unforgettable stories. Often we stumble on to a great story and tell ourselves: "Hey, no problem, I'll definitely remember that." But our lives are so busy that the story gets buried under a million other things in our memory. And lost forever. Write it down in your notebook before it slips out of your mind.

Don Murray and I were talking about bears. He told me about something that happened to him in Alaska. He walked into a store and saw a large dog sitting beside a man.

"Okay if I pet your dog?" Don asked.

"Sure," the man said, "but I won't."

"Why not?" Don asked.

"That's a bear dog," the man explained.

"A bear dog?" Don had never heard of that.

"I work out in the wilderness," the man told him. "My last three dogs were killed when a bear attacked. They stood up to a charging bear—that was how I managed to get away." He looked down at his dog. "Chances are, the same thing will happen to this feller. It's just too painful for me to get real attached to a good dog, and lose it. Go ahead and pet him. I won't. I try not to care too much about my dogs. It's just too painful."

TWO

Fierce Wonderings

As a boy I often visited Spy Pond when we went to see my grandmother in Arlington, Massachusetts. My mother grew up in Arlington. She had lots of stories about Spy Pond from her own child-hood—skating parties ·and picnics, as well as drownings.

"You've got to be careful when you swim in Spy Pond," she told me. "It's very deep. Some parts of it are bottomless."

"What do you mean, bottomless?"

"They haven't been able to find the bottom of the pond," she replied.

I ignored many things my mother said to me, but I could not ignore that word: *bottomless.* At night before going to sleep I'd chew it over in my mind. *Very deep*, sure, I could understand that. But I couldn't fathom (no pun intended) the idea of anything with no bottom. The very idea of it—*a bottomless pond*—gave me a bad case of the willies. I'd lie in bed imagining those murky depths, the cold water where no light ever penetrated. And I would ask myself questions: How could anything be bottomless? Did the water go down to the center of the earth? What was it like down there so deep?

It's important to pay attention to what haunts you, what images or memories keep running around in your mind even when you try not to think about them. But writing about what you wonder about isn't always as easy as it sounds. It takes honesty and courage. *Why do Dad and Mom fight like that? How can two people say they love each other and treat each other the way they do? Is this "love"?*

Brian Hamilton, a fourth grader in Ohio, spent time one day watching his grandmother. Afterward he wrote this entry in his notebook:

My Grandma Hayes sitting in her rocker with the knowledge of the last generation. Just makes you

*wonder how much she knows. For the past 80
years she has listened and thought and thought
some more. What does the world have in store?*

This kind of writing often gets you asking yourself big, open-ended questions that have no easy
answers. In her notebook, Mary Squillace, a
fourth grader, ponders the purpose of her life:

*Why was I born?
    Sometimes I think I'm going to be famous or
maybe I'll make a change in the world; I've got to
be around for something.*

Briana Carlin, a fifth grader from Long Island,
New York, uses her notebook to explore feelings
about being an adopted child:

*It's kind of hard being an adopted kid. You have so
many questions. As I look at my house I ponder . . .
Could I have had a better life? All I know is that
they would both love me.*

Like Mary, Briana begins to tackle major
questions about her identity: Who am I? Who are

my real parents? What is their life like? How is it different from the life I have?

Real wonder is hard to fake:

You know when you're looking down at an ant hole and you think there are about a zillion ants crawling around there in front of your eyes? Well I can compare that to my wonders. I have about a zillion wonders. I'll name some for you, but not too many, and not too less. I've always wondered about the moon—if a kind of creature lives on it. Or what are those little blue dents in it? I have also wondered about what if I had no friends? I mean what would I do at school? (I probably wouldn't go)—what would my life be like? I also wonder about my future. How many kids I'll have? What I'm going to be? I just wonder about so many things.

REBECCA HAFNER, fifth grade

Do I want to grow up?

I love being with my family, but I can't say that all the time. I really feel that when I am with my relatives there is no kid left in me. I am all grown up.

I have to help in the kitchen, baby-sit, and other responsibilities. At the time I feel great, a kind of feeling that I'm growing up, but later after it's all over I wonder do I really want to grow up that fast? Do I want all my childhood to be gone just like that? Is growing up as wonderful as people say it is? I look out at the world and see how tired grown-ups become and I think: Do I really want to throw all my childhood behind me? Do I really want to lose the feeling that I can always just crawl into my mother's lap and just wait until everything is better again? Do I . . . ?

ESTHER LIVINGSTONE, fifth grade

What do you wonder about? What's on your mind when you wake up? What do you daydream about at lunch or on the bus? What questions haunt or nag at you at night during those last moments before your consciousness crumbles and you fall asleep? You can explore these questions in your writer's notebook. They can be big scary questions *(What happens to the thinking part of me after I die?)*, but there are plenty of intriguing smaller questions to ponder, too:

- *They say that salmon always return to spawn in the same river they were born in. How can that be? After being in the ocean, how can they possibly find their way back?*
- *How can certain basketball players "hang" in the air? It doesn't make sense. I mean, doesn't everyone feel gravity in the same way?*

In her notebook, Kristi Storaekre, a New York fifth grader, wonders about a "conversation" between crows:

Birds (crows talking to each other):

I heard crows talking to each other. When I heard them I wanted to know what their conversation was. I didn't know if they were talking, calling, or fighting. I wish I could understand what they were saying.

You probably won't find easy answers to bottomless questions like these. In fact, you may explore them for years without finding answers that satisfy you. But that's all right. As a writer you need to know what you wonder about because this often leads to your best writing.

The writing you do about what you wonder about doesn't all have to be dead serious, either. Listen to this reflection by Joseph Powning, a fifth grader in Maine. You can tell that Joseph has been haunted by the immensity of the universe. But he manages to write about it in a style that is both serious and playful:

Have you ever thought of all that space, galaxy upon galaxy of inky black blackness? Where does it stop? Nowhere because nothing technically is something. If you keep thinking about it you'll go crazy! On and on an occasional star or planet. Ohhh! There are happy times that you forget all that and have fun. I like those times but ohhhhh! I can't get it out of my mind. Don't listen to this or you'll start thinking about it, too! Clamp your hands on your ears, make me stop, the wonders will infest us all! Forget I ever told you this! You may not think much now but later you'll be cursed with such thoughts. Just think: our world is a particle spinning through an infinity!

THREE

Writing Small

David is a fifth grader. After returning from vacation, he wrote this entry in his writer's notebook: "Cape Cod is the BEST. I had tons of fun there and I CAN'T WAIT TO GO BACK!!!!"

David and I talked about what he'd written.

"If you liked the Cape that much, you'll probably end up writing more entries about it," I said. I gave him a challenge: I suggested that the next time he wrote about Cape Cod, he try to describe exactly what it was that made it so terrific.

David did write another entry about Cape Cod. Notice the difference between this new entry and the first one he wrote.

Most nights we ate dinner right on the beach. We'd stay up late and I'd fall asleep still wearing my bathing suit. In the morning the first thing I felt when I woke up was my cat licking the salt off the soles of my feet.

That last salty detail really snaps Cape Cod into focus.

Maybe the single most important lesson you can learn as a writer is to *write small.* Use your writer's notebook to jot down the important little details you notice or hear about. These details make writing come alive. I have learned the hard way that I almost certainly forget them if I don't take a few minutes to write them down.

A single detail can sometimes give a window into a person's whole life. After my aunt Mary died, my relatives gathered to help clean out her house. Among Aunt Mary's belongings, my mother found several half-finished sketches of birds and plants. This surprised us; I don't think any of us knew my aunt had tried her hand at drawing.

This is exactly the kind of small detail I record

in my notebook. My aunt Mary lived a long life, and she was always good to me. But the sight of those unfinished drawings started me thinking. She never got married, and she spent many of her adult years living with and caring for her elderly mother. I wondered if maybe some of Aunt Mary's dreams had been unfinished, too.

The world is jam-packed with millions of details to notice; in your notebook you'll only have room for a tiny fraction. Try to select the ones that capture what's really important.

October 8

Boy, does Carol miss Colorado! She watches every Denver Bronco football game on TV (even though they're not very good this year). She's been living here in New Hampshire for two years but she still keeps her car clock set on Rocky Mountain time. Twice she's let me borrow her car but I always have to remind myself to subtract two hours to figure out what time it really is.

That one detail—Carol keeping the clock in her car set on Rocky Mountain time even though she lives in the Eastern time zone—tells me exactly how homesick she is. The following entry from my notebook is also about homesickness:

October 2

Bonnie told me a story: "I taught for twelve years in the island of Guam, in the South Pacific. And every year around the first of November a box would arrive in the mail. It always felt light as a feather when I picked it up, but I knew what it was: leaves. Colored autumn leaves. My sister, who lived in Pittsburgh, used to send me a box of lovely fall leaves every year. I'd open the box, dump them out, and spread those leaves all over the living room. They looked so beautiful. And then I'd start to cry."

I wanted to capture the picture of those colorful autumn leaves being strewn all over the living room floor in Guam, a tropical island where the leaves never change colors. That image tells me better than anything how much she's missing home. In the next entry, I write about something that happened to me, a small event from a typical summer day:

August 29

Today has just been "one of those days." Cutting the lawn, I almost ran over a tiny toad. Luckily I saw a little grey head sticking out from the grass. I was plenty hot, hungry, and in a bad mood, but I stopped the lawn mower and picked up the toad even though it didn't much like it. I carried it into the woods. The critter repaid the favor by peeing on my fingers!

Writing just "one of those days" wouldn't tell me very much about this day when I reread these words a few months from now. I took a moment to record some of the small details that gave this day its special feeling.

You can train yourself to notice the details around you. Use all your senses—the smell of your grandmother's kitchen, the funny faces your big sister makes while putting on her makeup, the way your cat's shadow looks different in the early morning than it does at noon, the difference between how your dad's cheeks feel from morning to night.

I often find myself using too many general

words in my writer's notebook: *good, nice.* These words don't give much of a picture as to exactly what was going on. When this happens, I stop and try to "crack open" these words by using specific examples.

Not—"My Grandpa is really nice" but "My Grandpa pulled out his chest of war stuff and let me try on his old uniform."

Not—"His mother is super neat" but "She irons everything, even her ten and twenty dollar bills!"

Not—"My Uncle Paul does lots of silly stuff" but "Uncle Paul drinks his coffee out of a glass measuring cup. On the way to the beach he stops at the fruit stand so he can buy corn and eat it raw."

You can do this yourself. Reread your writer's notebook and look for places where you are using vague, general words: *fun, cool.* Circle those words. Ask yourself: What are the details underneath these words? What little things will bring to life what I'm writing about? Write these details into your notebook. You don't even have to use complete sentences—a list will do.

In one junior high class, Anthony was writing

in his notebook about how lonely he used to feel as a kid. I asked him to think about what details he could use to help a reader picture this lonely feeling.

"I'm in my playroom and the light is off," Anthony wrote. "I pick a toy out of the toy box. At first I'm not sure what I'm holding but when it gets closer I can see exactly what it is—the hollow plastic telephone I use to call all my imaginary friends."

Write small. It makes a difference.

Joe, my car mechanic, came to the U.S. from Pakistan. This fellow is a wizard under the hood. Recently I tried to describe him in my writer's notebook. I could have written: *Joe really knows cars.* But a sentence like that is much too general and obvious to be any good. Instead, I decided to focus on his hands:

Joe has the most amazing hands. When I go to shake his hand after he's finished a job he smiles and backs away, apologizing that his hands are too dirty. And he's right; they are filthy, totally covered with grime with darker dirt under his fingernails. It's like his palms and thick fingers have been soaking for years in dirt, motor oil, and who knows what else. It would take a whole bar of heavy-duty soap, maybe two, and still I doubt those hands would ever come clean. But I love those hands; I'm glad they're filthy like that. Come to think of it, I'd get awfully nervous talking to a mechanic I could actually shake hands with.

Details like these will breathe life into your writer's notebook. Keep your eyes open and pay attention to little things that reveal important truths: hands, gestures, objects, anecdotes. Have fun with it. The small details or moments that end up in your writer's notebook don't have to be deadly serious ones, either.

January 22

Watched Adam play basketball this morning and something funny happened. There was a scramble for a loose ball. Adam came up with it, and started dribbling like crazy, but he was heading toward the wrong basket! Lucky for him a kid from the other team ran in front of him and started guarding Adam so Adam couldn't score on his own basket! I was laughing so hard my stomach hurt.

FOUR

Seed Ideas

Chicken eggs are pretty delicate. Fragile. Left on their own, without protection, these eggs would get stolen, eaten, or destroyed.

That's what incubators are for. An incubator creates conditions to give a chick the best possible chance to grow until one day it can peck its way out of the egg. Incubators have just the right moistness, the right temperature, the right brightness. In nature, the hen's body is a superb incubator. Hens even turn their eggs to make sure each part gets an equal amount of warmth.

A writer's notebook works just like an incubator: a protective place to keep your infant idea safe and warm, a place for it to grow while it is too young, too new, to survive on its own. In time you may decide to go back to that idea, add to it, change it, or combine it with another idea. In time the idea may grow stronger, strong enough to have other people look at it, strong enough to go out on its own.

Once in a while you get seized by an idea for a piece of writing—a poem, short story, play, or novel. That's one of the best uses for a notebook; it gives you a place to write down an idea before it wriggles out of your overloaded memory. It gives you a convenient place to keep the idea safe while it is still new.

A few months ago I was reading to my two-year-old son. He had chosen several books, including *Where the Wild Things Are* by Maurice Sendak. All at once a title for a book popped into my head: *Where the Wild Words Grow*, or maybe simply *Where the Words Grow*.

In a flash I could picture the book. I envisioned it as an illustrated book for readers somewhere around seven to ten. The main characters would be two children, maybe a brother and sister. They would wander out into the woods and chance upon a magical land or forest where words actually grow like fruit, vegetables, vines, or flowers. The children would meet someone—a man or "word wizard." (I liked the idea of a word wizard.) The wizard would show them how all the different words grow. I could imagine this word wizard explaining it to the children:

"See that field over there? That's where we grow the shortest words like I and a. That's a pretty hardy crop—doesn't need much rain. They'll grow just about anywhere, specially the I's . . .

"The verbs grow on those vines. Go ahead, help yourself, pick some if you want. Some of them are pretty tough—don't be afraid to *pull, yank, rip* them down. . . .

"That's a palindrome tree you're looking at—words like *radar* and *level*. You don't see many of those growing around here.

"See the ones over there, those colorful ones that look like flowers? Those are describing words. You should smell them!"

That was my idea for a book. It was no more than that—an idea—and maybe not a very good one at that. That's okay. I know that not every seed idea in my notebook will blossom into a piece of finished writing. But the idea excited me because I love words; it seemed like the book might be fun to write.

Some writers find it helpful to talk out an idea like this. I don't talk about it, not at first, anyway. I write it in my notebook. This is a special kind of fast writing where I almost never stop to look up a word and make sure I spell it right. At first my only goal is to get the idea down while it's still "hot." Often I leave space around the seed idea in my notebook, even an empty page or two, so I can later go back and add more to it. Here's what I wrote:

> Picture book idea—Where the Words Grow. Fantasy story about two kids (brother and sister?) who stumble upon a magical land where words grow. Ruled by a Word Wizard (title?) The O's bubble up from the ocean. The kids walk through thickets of dense, big words. The words grow back as soon as you pick them. Will there be a problem or conflict that needs to be resolved?

There! Now I can wait and be patient, knowing that at least I've got the main idea written down.

Some writers get an idea for a book and play around with the idea long before they try a first draft.

"When I can't seem to write, I write notes to get me going," says Katherine Paterson, author of *Bridge to Terabithia* and other books for young people. Paterson wrote these rambling notes about an idea for a book:

> What I am trying to do is write a book. But I can't start there. A little girl with sad brown eyes. She's worried and has no one to talk about her worry. Why? Probably the adults in her life have such enormous worries—worries she can't really understand but senses that in proportion hers will not be heard above the din. This is probably a school book. School always causes great anxieties. She is afraid of school. Is it a new school? a new teacher? Strange classmates. Very loud and seemingly much quicker smarter and more self-assured than she feels. What is the tone of the book? Does she have to protect a younger sibling in an unfriendly atmosphere? Takes off her barrette and scratches something into the red paint of the teacher's new car. She

doesn't have anything else chalk? magic marker? spray paint? to decorate with. She has fallen in love with her teacher and is heartbroken and angry when he tells the class he is going to get married. She has only begun to feel at home and to trust him.

These are the first notes for Katherine Paterson's novel *Flip-Flop Girl*. They are dated October 2, 1991, an entire year before she started writing the book. Katherine Paterson seems to have written these notes quickly, more concerned with figuring out what this book might be about than in getting all the commas and capital letters in the right place.

You can use your notebook to record any writing ideas you might have. Casey Dinkin, an eighth grader living in upstate New York, got an idea for a story based on people in her English class. She jotted these sketchy notes in her notebook:

Saga of an 8th grade English table
6 (5?) kids, different personalities, all in different

perspectives that switch back and forth.
Me
Rob
Popularity Queen, simple
Someone shy, quiet, complex
Wacko teacher
Philosophy assignment—get to know your own
and other's philosophy

The seed idea that Michael Abbondadolo, a fifth grader, wrote in his notebook was a memory involving his mother:

My Mom is very special. She makes me feel very safe. Whenever I had a bad dream or I was scared I'd go into my mom's room and hold her hair. That made me feel safe. I really don't do that anymore but I know my mom is a very special person.

Much later he returned to that entry and used it as the starting place for a memoir, which is a longer piece of autobiographical writing. Note how Michael expanded the original entry for his memoir:

Scared

Ah Ah Ah Ah Ah. . . . It happened again. My bad dream. One night it was "JAWS," another night it was a ghost, now it's a witch.

"Ah Ah Ah Ah Ah. . . !" I screamed. I woke up and looked around. It was dark and scary. Very quickly I zoomed into my mother's room, almost falling down the stairs.

I jumped into mid-air over the bed and landed on my dad's leg and crawled into the middle and hugged my mom. My dad on one side, my mother on the other, I was in the middle. I felt like it was a force-field. Nothing could get past, not even the witch. I was safe with my mom. I was afraid to go to sleep, but I just held my mom's hair and then I fell asleep.

Often you can find a newspaper article that gives you an idea for something you might write. A few years ago I read a published letter from a mother whose five-year-old daughter had a bad habit of shoplifting. When the mother found out the first time, she dragged the girl back to the store and begged the owner to punish her. But the girl charmed the owner, and he gave her a gentle scolding instead of punishment. This happened again and again. One time the mother pleaded with the store owner to call the police. But the policeman took a liking to the girl; he didn't punish her either. I wrote this down in my notebook—it struck me as an interesting premise for a story.

In another newspaper I found a long article about the flooding of rivers. In the article I learned one intriguing fact—a river tends to flood over the area originally followed before being moved by dams and levees. I copied this fact into my notebook. Later, it would be the catalyst for a poem:

How Rivers Flood

Bad news in Current Events:
you flirting with Judd Roth
while Mr. Hunt drones on
about natural disasters:

"When a river floods it
remembers its old path,
the one it used to follow
before dams and levees."

He calls on me. I shrug.
Who cares about rivers,
you, these dark waters
rising fast inside me?

Do ideas for stories or poems or plays ever flit into your head? Well, now you can bring them into one central place where you know they'll be safe until you need them. Use your writer's notebook as a specimen box to collect ideas—even strange, surprising, far-fetched ideas. Don't censor yourself. But don't expect these "seeds" to sprout immediately, either. Wait. A writer needs patience. Many writers find that their seed ideas have to sit in the notebook for a long time, even years, before they start to take root in the imagination.

Paul Fleischman, author of *Joyful Noise* and *Bull Run*, has kept a notebook since his high school days. One day he wrote in his writer's notebook: *Traveling school teacher, boarding around.*

"This was the germ behind the young school teacher in *The Borning Room*," Fleischman says. "That book was written about *twelve years* after I wrote this note."

Thoughts about Notebooks from Paul Fleischman

As a writer, Paul Fleischman seems to do it all—novels, poetry, picture books, nonfiction. My favorite Paul Fleischman novels are *Bull Run* and *The Borning Room*. His book of poems for two voices, *Joyful Noise*, won the Newbery Medal Award in 1989. Paul Fleischman lives in Pacific Grove, California.

I do keep a notebook. In it I have sections devoted to ideas for stories, characters, descriptions, scenes, titles, names (male, female, last), as well as facts picked up from books and newspapers that might serve me someday. I'm always adding to it. When I'm finished with a book and thinking of starting another, I go through it and select the ideas that give me the most voltage. Often I've forgotten that I've written an idea in the notebook, and will later find that it appears 2 or 3 times; those are the ideas that usually become books, ideas that tug at your sleeve for years.

The road from notebook entry to book is usually a long one. Most of my ideas lie in the notebook for several years—sometimes as long as 10 or 15—before being drawn on. Most of what's in there will never be used. A writer never knows exactly what he or she will need in the future; you jot things down that seem pressing at the moment, knowing that, as with a dream, they may fade in the future morning's light.

I've kept a notebook since high school. I began with a tiny wire-bound notebook, which I still have, which is one of the great advantages of notebooks: they let you keep your ideas. Having written my books, like my notebooks, with a pencil on paper, I like being able to tell students that everything they need to be a writer will fit in their shirt pocket: a small notebook and a pen and pencil. I much prefer them to computers; the pencil and notebooks are portable, inexpensive, unobtrusive, and not vulnerable to "crashing" or power outages.

FIVE

Mind Pictures

There is some lovely country near our house here in New Hampshire. You don't have to walk far before you come upon grassy meadows with cows and horses. Not long ago our baby-sitter, a college senior named Krista, took my son Joseph out for a walk in his stroller.

"Nice walk?" I asked when she returned.

"Oh, yeah! I love that old overturned VW bug. Looks like it's just sort of melting into that pasture."

"Right," I said. But I thought: What buggy? What on earth was she talking about?

The next day I put Joseph in the backpack and left the house. This time I was looking for the car, and sure enough, I saw it, just past a ramshackle barn, lying on its back exactly as Krista had said. The car was white and rusty, with grass grown up around it. Where had it come from? How many times had I made the same walk without ever noticing it? How could I have missed it?

I took a mental photograph of the car and continued my walk. When I returned to the house I wrote a quick description in my notebook: *VW bug, abandoned, lying on its back in the meadow.*

Now whenever I took this walk I always noticed that car. I began wondering about it. Where had it come from? Who drove it last? How had it ended up turned over in that pasture? A year later I decided to write a poem about it:

beetle

Who knows the story
behind this VW Bug
white and well-rusted,

utterly abandoned
to a meadow of weeds
and wild blackberries?

Who knows how it got
turned on its back
tires pointed up

like an unlucky beetle
who never learned to
turn back over?

Pay attention to your world. Wherever you are,
at all hours of the day, try to drink in the world
through your five senses, all of which are incredibly important tools for a writer. And when something strikes you that you want to remember,
make time to scribble at least a quick description
of it in your notebook.

Step one: *Pay attention.* Be ready. Keep your
senses peeled.

Step two: *Write down what you notice before you
forget.*

Step three: *Later, go back and reread your entry.
See if you might want to write more about it.*

Too often we don't pay enough attention to
what's around us. I must have walked by that overturned VW bug forty or fifty times without seeing

it! I was walking outside, but I might just as well have been strolling through a mall. Maybe I was preoccuppied or in a bad mood. For whatever reason, my eyes were open but I didn't see.

You can start paying attention to your world by squeezing some of the junk out of your head. Try to clear out enough mental garbage (worries, unfinished projects, the "cool" girl who snubbed you in the cafeteria, the easy shot you missed in the basketball game) so you can be in the world and breathe in what's around you. The goal of a writer is to be a sponge.

> We went to York Beach yesterday late in the after-noon. Great day, clear and sunny. The beach was at low tide with a strong on-shore wind. The sand was dark with dry, lighter sand blowing over it. The dry sand made ghostly white ribbons that snaked down to the water.

Keeping a writer's notebook can help you be more alive to the world. It can help you develop the habit of paying attention to the little pictures and images of the world you might otherwise ignore.

When you describe a mind picture in your notebook, don't feel like you always have to write a long entry with complete sentences and neat print. Write down just enough so that, later, rereading the words will reawaken the image in your imagination. Even a few words—*ribbons of sand at York Beach*—will usually do the trick.

Not long ago I went out to walk to think through a problem I was having with a close friend. Halfway through my walk I came upon a large black dog I had never seen before. He was standing in the middle of the road, as if waiting for me, and he didn't move or wag his tail as I got closer. I saw his broad chest. I saw the eyes glittering at me with no shred of warmth. And no shred of fear. I tried to stay relaxed because I had read somewhere that dogs can smell fear on a person. (How does fear smell? Sweet? Putrid?) I didn't want that dog to smell any fear on me.

"Hey, feller," I said as I drew even with the dog. *Grrr!* He barked once, head snapping around to watch me as I walked by. I had to force my feet to continue walking calmly, eyes forward, even though I was dying to look back.

When I passed that menacing dog I felt a

gigantic wave of relief. My shirt was damp with sweat. I took a deep breath and went back to think about the problem I'd been worrying about, only now it didn't seem like such a big deal. When I returned home I wrote in my notebook a short entry about this incident: *big dog—cleansed by fear.* Those five words would be enough to remind myself of what had happened.

As you pay closer attention to the world around you, consider playing the *that-looks-like* or *that-sounds-like* game. It's a game you can play with any of your senses. I say *play* because it's fun to compare two objects (a fire hydrant and a toddler in a red snowsuit) that don't seem to have much in common. These comparisons allow you to stretch and play with the images you collect in your notebook.

April 24

Spring finally coming! I saw the forsythia today, bright yellow petals clustered thick around the branches. Like concentrated sunlight. I saw three bushes in front of a house and when the breeze blew I had a vision of three girls with golden curls wearing frilly ruffled yellow dresses. Their curls and

48

dresses fluttered in the the warm breeze like yellow flames.

May 3

Last night I rode my bike up Sumac Lane. On the way I passed an old house. In front there were two mailboxes leaning against each other. It looked like a real old couple dancing slowly cheek-to-cheek.

Use your notebook to capture the mind "photographs" you take of the world around you. In his notebook, fifth grader Jerry Hollenbeck describes his cat's love of tree-climbing:

Black Climbing

My cat Blacky loved to climb trees. Almost every day Blacky would be right up a tree when he went out. He was a good cat. Sometimes Blacky would just take his sweet old time climbing a tree. But when I was up a tree he would book it up that tree. Blacky just loved birds. When he heard a bird he would race up and cuddle with them. When Blacky wasn't climbing he'd be in the house with me.

In her notebook, fifth grader Kristi Storaekre plays around with this image of her wet hair:

Snakes, that's what my hair looks like when it's wet, squiggling this way and that trying to get off my head but they can't because they're stuck.

Surprise images like this can make the reader sit up and pay attention. This is exactly the kind of thing that brings writing alive. You'll notice that Jerry and Kristi didn't have to go far to find their mind pictures; they chose something close to home. Evagelia, a writer in the fifth grade, does something similar when she uses words to paint a vivid picture of a favorite doll in this poem she wrote in her notebook:

My Little Doll

Stop staring at
me Christina
you're so precious
to me. When
I look at
Christina she's

so beautiful
with her elegant
dress and her golden hair
and sky blue eyes.
I wish I looked
like you Christina.

In her notebook, Heather Petruzzi describes the way her mother looks while reading a book. Notice the careful attention to detail:

As I watch my mommy, bent over into a book, I feel as if she's lost. Her face is always in the same position even though she switches off from biting her nails to putting her hand under her chin to just sitting there. Sometimes she turns her head or puts it down or up for a second, but that doesn't last much longer than that. From the way she looks I think that she's not fond of the book, but is reading it because she should. The book that she is reading is on education. To me that book would probably be quite boring, or least that's a guess. Oh well. Sunken into the couch, reading is at least comfortable and as I sit beside my mom, I feel like nothing in the world is going to hurt me. My Mom!

Sight is a crucially important tool to a writer. But the senses of smell, touch, sound, and taste are just as important. Rebecca Scefonas, a fifth grader in New York, uses her notebook to record the way high heels sound when a woman walks:

> High heels clicking. It sounds like ice cubes falling lightly. I thought it was a nice sweet sound. Not much noise, just a nice one.

As you read the following notebook entry by Brian Guptill, a fifth grader, notice how many senses he uses to describe winter:

> The snow is coming in and the birds have left. The cold and snowy air has taken over, making the ground icy and wet. The snowflakes small and large are covering the rivers and lakes and forests, rooftops and driveways. The plows are going back and forth up and down the roads making a scraping sound. Nightfall comes and an owl goes out flying for a small mouse. Some moose come looking for food in the field and they eat. The cool breeze numbs my cheek and face and I sit in the snow and think about winter.

Patricia Hubbell has published five books of poetry for young readers. When Patricia became interested in writing a book of poems about horses, she visited an equestrian center in Westport, Connecticut. There she spent a great deal of time observing horses and taking notes. Here are some of the images she jotted in her notebook:

The breeze, like a white horse canters the hill
But the wind is a black horse neighing
                            delicate
the breeze is a colt with ~~tripping~~ hooves
But the wind is a stallion calling
a horse muscled like a
river at flood time
                     a bay with four white socks
a long-backed
muscle-packed
high-hipped
never-nipped
family horse

Patricia Hubbell wrote many pages of notes like this. They eventually became poems for her anthology of horse poems, *A Green Grass Gallop*.

You can collect mind pictures wherever you are: the city sidewalk, YMCA, church, train station, pet store. Use all your senses. Try to describe as carefully and honestly as you can. Each house has its own distinct smell: exactly how would you describe the smell of your grandmother's house? What does it feel like when you gently squeeze your great grandfather's hand? How would you describe the feel and taste of hot apple pie and cold vanilla ice cream in your mouth?

DREAMS

One morning my four-year-old son came into bed, whimpering.

"What's wrong?" I asked. "Have a bad dream?"

"Yeah, Daddy," Robert sobbed softly. "I had a nightmirror."

"You mean a nightmare?" I asked, smiling to myself.

"Yeah," he said. "Some bad guys with no eyes were trying to get me."

I soothed Robert and sent him back to bed. But the word he'd spoken—*nightmirror*—echoed in my mind. He'd invented that word purely by accident but it occurred to me that this is exactly what a dream or nightmare really is: a nightmirror that reflects events, objects, and people from real life and distorts them in strange and disturbing ways.

3/13

Dreamed *last night I was in a house, old house (our house, maybe? we always lived in old houses) with some people from my family. I walked into the living room and was suddenly attacked by a swarm of black grasshoppers. They clung to my arms and legs and bit me. I screamed. Then some of the grasshoppers turned into birds. "Don't worry," my brother Jim said, "the birds will eat the grasshoppers." And they did. Later I went back to the living room and there were holes and pock-marks in the walls and ceilings where birds' beaks had bitten in their frenzied search for grasshoppers.*

Many of us wake up with dream fragments or dream images lingering in our heads. As a writer, try to get in the habit of writing down those dreams before they flit forever out of your head. Some people keep a "dream journal" and make a habit of recording their dreams each morning. Dreams or nightmares often contain unexpected twists and surprises that can provide invaluable material for your writing.

Many people drift through life. Your writer's notebook can work as an alarm clock to remind you to wake up and pay attention to what's happening in your world, both inside and out. There's nothing more important you can learn as a writer.

SIX

Snatches of Talk

Whenever my grandma Annie had a birthday, it gave my family an excuse to throw a big party that usually turned into a family reunion. When fully assembled, the Collins clan numbered well over a hundred uncles, aunts, cousins, second cousins. . . . We had the makings of a real blast when we all got together.

On Grandma's ninetieth birthday, we rented a big beach house on Cape Cod. Grandma sat in a folding chair under a shady tree not too far from the ocean. She had a lovely new dress on, and her eyes were bright and happy. I was standing nearby when my Uncle John approached.

"Happy birthday, Mother!" he cried, bending over to hug her.

"Hello, Billy!" she beamed back. "It's wonderful to see you."

"It's not Billy," Uncle John said. He looked confused. "It's Johnny. You know me, don't you, Ma?"

"Well, I haven't seen Johnny in a long time," she said. My uncle knelt beside Grandma and spoke to her softly: "Don't you know your son Johnny?"

"Couple years now, I think it is," Grandma said.

I stood there, listening, unable to move. Uncle John had fought in World War II and in the Korean War. I knew he had sent home money for Grandma month after month even when he didn't have much to send. I wondered if he would go get his brother Billy to clear up Grandma's confusion, but he didn't, not then. Instead he gave her a sad look.

"Mother, you look terrific," he said, smiling and touching her cheek. "You have yourself a great day, all right? And when you do see Johnny, remember to give him my love. I know he's been asking for you."

Grandma Annie is no longer alive, but I remember this moment like it happened yesterday, because I wrote it down in my writer's notebook. The scene cut at my heart: Grandma Annie, an energetic mother of eight children, unable to recognize her own son, the words passed between mother and son, the pain on my uncle's face, the sad, stiff way he held his body when he walked away. I tried to put myself in his shoes. How would that feel? If my own mother didn't know me, how could I be sure who I really was?

Writers are fascinated by talk, obsessed with what people say and how they say it, how they interrupt themselves, the words they repeat, the way they pronounce or mispronounce certain words. The way we talk says a ton about who we are. My notebooks are filled with dialogue: snatches of talk or arguments between strangers, relatives, and friends:

Mom describing a restaurant:
   "The place was so clean you could've eaten off the floor."

My brother Tom putting tons of black pepper on his scrambled eggs:
   "I want it to look like a coal miner sneezed on it!"

Ever since my son Robert started talking, I have collected the weird, funny, wise things that have come out of his mouth:

We took a ride on the ferry. I walked with Robert (just three) to the top of the boat where a couple dozen people were standing around. A sunny windy day.

"Look, Daddy," he said, pointing at the people. "Everybody's puffing up!"

He was right! In the strong wind, people's shirts and jackets and blouses looked all "puffed up," filled with air.

For years novelist Jackie French Koller wrote down selected things her children said. One day her son Devin said: "Maybe if you thought you were pretty, you would be."

Jackie wrote down this line in her notebook. Later she used this idea in her novel *A Place to Call Home*. Another time, Jackie said to a friend on the telephone: "I can't wait to see Heather. I hear she's grown another foot."

Jackie's five-year-old daughter Kerri overheard this. A week later, when Kerri saw Heather, she exclaimed: "You lied, Mommy! She didn't grow another foot! She still has only two!"

In Jackie's novel *For Impy for Always*, two characters say almost the exact same thing in the first chapter.

You can find many tasty morsels of talk in school. Check out this dialogue I overheard between two kindergarten boys:

"Know where molten lava comes from?" Benjamin asks another boy. Benjamin is an expert on volcanoes.

"The fire station?" Adrien asks, shrugging. He doesn't have a clue.

"The fire station!!" Benjamin cries, slapping his forehead. He rolls his eyes and looks at me. "No way! Do you know where molten lava comes from?"

"Well, the inside of the earth is filled with molten lava," I reply.

"The center of the earth is molten lava," he corrects me impatiently.

Keep your ears alert to the conversations of strangers wherever you are and pay attention to what strikes you. You don't need to write down the whole conversation; often you end up writing just a sentence or phrase in your notebook.

A woman at the supermarket talking to her son:
"Remember, Skip, tomorrow's a D-O-H-O."
"Huh?"
"A Day of Holy Obligation," she explained. "You have to go to church."
"Ohh," the boy groaned.

On a bus, a girl maybe five, talking to her father:
"Daddy, I saw a dog sleeping by the side of the road!"
"I don't think so, honey," the man told her softly. "Dogs don't sleep by the side of the road."

You can train yourself to develop an "ear for dialogue" as you listen to people's talk. Most of us tend to listen to what someone is *trying* to say. The trick is to listen hard enough to get the words that actually come out of that person's mouth.

Girls arguing about animal fur in junior high cafeteria:

"What's so bad about wearing fur?" one girl asks loudly. "Sheesh! We, like, eat meat and eggs, right? We use animals all the time. As long as they're not, like, becoming extinct—"

"I don't eat eggs or meat!"

"Maybe you should!" the first girl shouts back, thrusting out a hamburger to the other girl. "Go ahead: eat it! I eat anything that doesn't eat me!"

People have many original ways of expressing themselves. Use your notebook to collect the odd or unexpected things people say, such as my brother talking in his sleep:

Last night Jim opened his eyes in the middle of the night and started talking. He said:

"It's hard to sleep with sand on your feet and a candle in your hair."

"Huh?" I laughed. "What the heck are you talking about?"

"If you fold the candle, it doesn't go to sleep." He yawned, turned over, and went back to sleep.

• In the May 5, 1995 edition of the Wall Street

Journal page A6, I read an article about volleyball player Kent Steffes. This is how the author described him: "In beach lingo, he's a stoked-up big banger with pure smoke and a buff bod."

- In New Hampshire, people say the roads are "greasy" when the weather warms up and the snowy roads turn to slush. If a restaurant is too crowded, some people say it's "all bombed out."

- Whenever my son Adam sees a comic book or Magic card he admires, he'll say: "Sweet!" or "Sweetness!" and let out a low whistle of appreciation.

- We spent nine days in Anchorage, Alaska. We stayed with my friend Mike McCormick and his family. Mike described one of his favorite restaurants to us. "But I better warn you," Mike said. "That place is noisy, crowded, and real spendy (expensive)!"

- In Alaska I met a man who told me about a friend of his who had crashed his small airplane. "He didn't get hurt," the man said, "but his plane got tore up real bad. I'm telling you, he really crinkled that puppy!"

- *While bicyling through Ireland I was struck by the way people describe the ordinary things around them. I visited one town where the clouds looked dark and threatening. "Think it's going to rain?" I asked one man at a pub. He smiled and replied with a lilting voice: "Oh, just a touch of moisture to keep down the dust, you know."*

Try this. Go to a public place and sit quietly. After a few minutes, people will ignore you and start talking again as if you're not there. Listen. Listen to the cadences of ordinary talk, the rhythms of everyday speech. Later you can write down any memorable lines you heard.

Learn to listen wherever you go. Your notebook is the perfect place to record the funny or disturbing things you overhear on the playground, the words spoken by a tired mother at the mall, or the complaints of a first grader who doesn't want to go to school. Later, when you reread your notebook looking for writing ideas, you'll find this dialogue invaluable.

Collecting snatches of talk isn't an idle hobby. Many writers find that human talk provides crucial raw materials for their writing.

"When we have difficulty thinking of a beginning for a piece of writing, we may struggle to come up with a line out of our own minds," says poet Naomi Shihab Nye. "We might do better to start with a line we have heard, letting it be an invitation into the piece of writing."

Human talk has an amazing ability to capture a whole world in a few words. This is a dialogue I overheard between three boys who were each playing a handheld GameBoy:

"Goodbye, sucker!"

"Yaaaa! You're gone!"

"Ya got blood on your face—big disgrace! Nasty!"

"I'm dead. Shoot! I always die on Level Eight. I musta died a million times on Level Eight."

"I'm wicked awesome. Hey, lemme—no wait! Watch this!"

"I hate Level Eight! I'm sick of dying! C'mon, teach me not to die!"

"Wait a sec, I gotta waste this guy. Ha! Goodbye!"

Thoughts about Notebooks from Naomi Shihab Nye

The poems of Naomi Shihab Nye have been enjoyed by readers young and old all over the world. Her books include *The Yellow Glove, Sitti's Secrets,* and *This Same Sky, A Collection of Poems from around the World.* Naomi Shihab Nye lives in San Antonio, Texas.

Writing in a notebook is a way to fuel up. Supreme superior unleaded. And it's free.

We think, "I'll remember that." But it's not true. So much would have been lost if we weren't writing details down in a notebook. When I read old entries it's as if I've kept a map to all the people I used to be. Wasn't she silly? Wasn't she an oddball? And here's the old woman in the pink housecoat whose name I never knew watering her crepe myrtle bushes with a hose every day at exactly 7:30 A.M.! Suddenly I have so many friends.

When our son was born, my friend Kim Stafford gave me a lovely handmade notebook in which to write details about Madison's early years and record his sayings. This is the very best present you could ever give any person about to become a parent. Of all my notebooks, the Madison notebooks are my greatest treasure. I quickly realized I could do nothing but record what Madison did and still feel like a poet.

Since Madison started speaking quite clearly even before he turned one, that notebook got full very quickly. His first sentence, when he was an eleven-month-old baby in diapers lying on the bed, was "Daddy, bed hot, off." I made a long list of all the words he could say by his first birthday. Would I have remembered them without the notebooks? No way! I might have remembered five or ten.

I got another notebook.
And another and another.

Many of Madison's quotes have worked their way into stories and poems and essays. I've even done a few "found poems"—nothing but his own words arranged by me. He said them, I inscribed them, and "found" them later in my notebook.

I have also kept notebooks of things other people say—even people I don't know, in airports, on trains. Students in lunch lines at school. Sometimes these quotes are very mysterious, or intriguing, and will lead us somewhere else. I have a whole notebook filled with quotes by an old friend of mine named Kerry, one of the best talkers I ever knew. When we have difficulty thinking of a beginning for a piece of writing, we may struggle to come up with a line out of our own minds, an idea, when we might do better to start with a line we have heard, letting it be an invitation into the piece.

Rereading notebooks is like reliving your life. I think they're more important than money in the bank.

You might write a line down today that you don't "use" in a piece of writing for years! Or, you might never "use" it at all. But just getting in the habit of writing little things all the time helps sharpen your perceptions. Can you imagine a star athlete never exercising or warming up! Notebooks are a stretch, a jog around the block.

Don't think of a notebook as "duty" or "work"—think of it as play. Remember when you were little and might wander around outside just picking up whatever looked interesting at the moment, maybe even putting it in your pocket—a shaggy grass, a twig that looked like the letter Y. Your notebook still has room for all those things. It's better than a pocket because no one will have to wash it later.

Some people like to keep different things. For years I put all my dreams in a notebook with a wooden cover from Finland. It smelled dreamy, for one thing, like a cedar closet stacked with sweaters. I kept it by my bed with a pen stuck in it. I don't write all my dreams down anymore—just a few of them. Many poems used to begin with a line from a dream. Now I really like tiny portable note-books. You can make your own out of folded typing paper—cheap! Kim Stafford taught me that, too. He keeps his full little notebooks filed in shoeboxes with dates on them. He can say, "Now what was I thinking that summer in Idaho?" and know just where to find it. I am not as well-organized. I have to dig every-where to find something. But I usually find forgotten surprises along the way.

SEVEN

Lists

What is it about lists? Maybe it's the need humans have to accumulate stuff. Maybe it's the urge to catalogue our immense, mysterious world. For whatever reason, many writers keep lists: favorite books, movies to see, ideas for all sorts of writing projects. And the writer's notebook is the ideal place to keep them.

Sara Mae Zerner, a fifth grade writer in Manhasset, New York, keeps a writer's notebook. In it she keeps a list of her favorite words, a list she adds to whenever she finds a new word she likes:

zap   *giggles*
Zimbabwe   *glimmering*

zombie	cactus
zit	crunch
Zelda	Colorado
penguin	dolphins
banana	couplet

Another boy in Sara's class keeps a similar list of his best words, which includes *chunky, funky, onomatopoeia, pog, wigwam.* I do exactly the same thing. For years I have kept a section at the rear of my writer's notebook for favorite words:

persnickety
succatash — *Both fun words to say.*

chimichanga — *I love the music of*
tse-tse fly — *these words, especially*
Boutros Boutros-Ghali — *how they repeat parts.*

Scuppernong — *Grapes that grow wild in Mississippi.*

calabash

crescendo

quicksand — *The idea of it has always terrified me.*

osprey	*Killer bird—I love how the word prey hides inside.*
counterintuitive	*Cool word!*
light sweet crude	*A category of oil. The phrase always makes me smile because light and sweet don't seem to fit with crude.*
chemical incapacitants	*Mace, for instance. Not a word to mess around with.*
stressed=desserts spelled backward	*I'm wild about palindromes.*
jimmy the lock	*I have a brother named Jimmy. I've always been fascinated that the word could also be a verb.*

Whenever I come across an unusual new word, I add it to my list. It can't be just any old word—it has to be new or remarkable in some way. You can do this yourself. In your notebook, start your own list of favorite or new words. Think of it as adding new tools to your writer's toolbox. Look for the chance to use these new words in all your writing.

I keep other kinds of lists that have personal importance to me. For example, when our sons began to talk, I kept a list of all the words they could say. And I added to these lists until the words could no longer fit on one page.

For New Year's Eve, you might make a list of wishes for the new year. Tape your list into your writer's notebook. Next New Year's Eve you can look back to see which wishes came true. (Some do.)

You might also make a list of writing projects or ideas you want to write about. One way I do this is to make a list of possible titles:

Ghost of a Chance
Needle and a Threat
Filthy Rich
They Don't Have Fireflies in Aspen

The notebook is also a place to give yourself deadlines; set goals:

Writing Goals for End of Summer

1. Finish *Notebook* book
2. Finish *Ordinary Things*
3. Revise *Spider Boy*
4. Revise two picture book manuscripts
5. Write at least ten flower poems
6. Write draft of article for *New Advocate*

Louise Borden, author of several picture books for children, uses her notebook to keep track of her goals. Here's a page from her notebook listing titles for books she hopes to write:

The Little Ships
River Camp
Cursive
Lindbergh Biplane
The Five Run Homer

You might also list the individual parts of a writing project. This works as a kind of brainstorming that helps you think through what you're working on. Two years ago, I started listing as many family stories as I could remember:

1. Jessie (kid from Fresh Air program who spent the summer with us)
2. Dancing lessons (from the girl across the street)
3. War with firecrackers
4. Spencer (neighborhood bully)
5. Tackle Box story
6. No-Beak (seagull with no beak)
7. The crystal mumbo-jumbo (prized marble)
8. Fire-Bug! (my brother the pyromaniac)
9. Time Bobby saw Santa Claus
10. Making stollen with Grandma
11. Under the kitchen table

Some of these stories became the basis for my novel *Fig Pudding.*

You can use your notebook to list unusual scientific or historical facts. For instance, spiders have always fascinated me. For years my notebooks have contained lists of spider facts and trivia collected from wherever I could find them.

Spider experts estimate that the insects eaten by spiders in one year would weigh more than fifty million people!

Spiders eat mostly insects. But also fish and amphibians, lizards, young snakes. Even birds and small animals.

Most spiders use webs to catch their prey, but not all. Jumping spiders don't use any webs at all. They stalk their prey slow and secret as a cat.

There's one kind of spider (Mimetus) who lives by eating only other spiders.

Spiders get eaten by small birds, and are often fed to baby birds still in the nest. Many birds like to use spider's egg cocoons to line their nests.

Man is the biggest threat to spiders. People. We cut down rainforests where they live. We capture them and sell them as pets. We use too much insecticides in farming—that poisons spiders.

Spiders are eaten by people in many parts of the world! The native people of Laos eat two different types of big spiders. They are roasted, dipped into salt. Legs pulled off. Supposedly the *abdomen tastes like raw potato and lettuce mixed. Yum!*

Listing facts like this is one of the best ways I know to brainstorm about a subject that interests you. Not long ago I spent five solid hours weeding my vegetable garden. During that time I got the urge to write about weeds. I wrote the word "Weeds" on the top of a blank notebook page and began generating thoughts connected to this subject. When I "freewrite" like this, I try to just let my thoughts flow without censoring my imagination:

Picture book by Aliki—A Weed Is a Flower What makes a weed a weed?
  Little kids don't know the difference between real flowers and weed flowers. Do bees?
  Are weeds naughty flowers?
  Weeds have super deep roots—they grow back if you don't cut out the whole root.

I collected weed ideas, on and off, for a few days before I started to write. After several drafts, here's what I got:

Weeds

Weeds blossom
just like flowers.

A weed is a flower
with a bad attitude.

Weeds and real flowers
attract bees about equally.

Weeds are just garden flowers
who don't put on any fancy airs.

Bees don't distinguish between garden
flowers or weeds so long as they're sweet.

In even the most carefully weeded garden
at least one weed will find a way to slip inside.

Weed roots go down real deep. If you don't dig out
the roots of this poem I guarantee it will grow back.

If you are a list-lover, consider keeping your lists in a writer's notebook. Brainstorm what sorts of lists you might want to make. Leave room at the end of each list so you can add to it as you come up with new ideas. Don't be afraid to include some fun lists: favorite (or worst) foods, important firsts in your life, pet peeves. Rob van Alstyne, an eighth-grade writer in upstate New York, keeps a list of his favorite quotes and one-liners, which includes:

1. *In the land of the blind the one-eyed man is king.*
2. *When elephants fight the grass suffers.*
3. *He who increases knowledge increases suffering.*

Lately I have begun the following list in my writer's notebook:

Little Things That Irritate Me

1. **Crumbs in the butter:** *after someone has buttered their toast the stick of butter has all these disgusting little crumbs in it!*
2. **When a building drips on you:** *walking under an awning or air-conditioning unit when a glob of sickly warm toxic liquid falls on my head.*

3. **Stickered fruit/vegetables:** *buying individual apples, tomatoes, or avocadoes that have little paper stickers on them you have to peel off.*

4. **Ads for "free" stuff:** *let's face it—it's never "free." There's always a catch.*

Casey Dinkin is an eighth-grade writer from New York. Her notebook has her own list of "Gripes":

1. _____ *really annoys me.*
2. *I never get to sleep early enough.*
3. *I'm so undecided.*
4. *Life is so inexplainable.*
5. *Why can't people recognize great music? Today for ART I brought my Beatles tape to listen to. I bet they'd all rather hear Green Day.*

Thoughts about Notebooks
from Louise Borden

Louise Borden has written a number of books, including the *Watching Game, Albie the Lifeguard*, and *Just in Time for Christmas*. She lives in Terrace Park, Ohio, with her husband, three children, and lots of writer's notebooks.

> *All these are parts of a working writer's notebook: photographs, quotes, the language of other writers, newspaper clippings, letters from research, personal letters (written and received), daily entries, struggling rough drafts. . . .*

> *Most of my notebooks are black/white composition books. I also have several larger notebooks . . . binders with pockets and various sections. I gathered all my journals and notebooks I've kept since 1984 and began reading through them. This is what I discovered:*

- I tended to focus on the same subjects: family, writing/publishing, friendship, landscape/place, and reflections on school visits
- I used the same voice in many reflective entries
- there was a repetitiveness in many entries
- I set goals in writing . . . small steps scattered throughout the notebooks
- I wrote about faith and belief in my book projects as well as the doubt and difficulties encountered in these projects
- family, writing, and friends seem to be at the heart of my personal and professional lives
- some of the writing seemed average and some lines seemed powerful and full of heart

I write daily on white lined tablets . . . long letters to close professional friends, observations and thoughts about the many schools I visit, and descriptions of place. It is a habit, this kind of writing, this trying to make order and sense of those subjects closest to me. When I write on these tablets, covering a smooth white page with ink and words, I am always surprised by what I learn . . . each sentence opens a door that can make familiar thoughts new. This kind of writing never fails to lead me to new places.

EIGHT

Memories

Memories just may be the most important posses-
sion any writer has. As much as anything else, our
memories shape what we write. Memories are like
a fountain no writer can live without. I believe
that my best writing springs from that fountain.

As a writer, you need to connect yourself with
your own unique history. Claim it as your own.

When I graduated from college I wanted badly
to be a writer. I thought I had to have wild adven-
tures so I'd have something to write about. It
never occurred to me that locked in my memory
I already had almost everything I would need for
my first novel.

In my writer's notebook I often go back,

spading into the soil of my past life, trying to unearth the person I once was. When I write about a memory I try to capture it as honestly and accurately as possible.

The first house I really remember was in Marshfield, Massachusetts, on Ocean Street. Downstairs there was a floor heater that took up most of the hallway. The heater got hot so you had to scrunch against the wall so you wouldn't touch the metal grating when you walked by on bare feet.

The kitchen had a linoleum floor. There were six large black squares, each with a white square in the middle. At night, after bath time and just before bed, the five kids in our family would sit on the floor. Mom would give us a cookie and a cup of milk. Such a cozy feeling, sitting on the floor, each of us on our own square, eating a snack before bed.

When we came out of the restaurant, I saw a man cutting the grass about twenty feet from our car. The windshield of our car looked like it had a bright round spiderweb on it. Cracked! Dad swore softly and walked over to the man cutting the lawn. The other man killed the engine.

"Did you do that?" Dad asked angrily. He pointed at his windshield.

"I didn't think so . . ." the man said. "Must've hit a rock or something. Sorry."

"Well, someone's going to pay for this," Dad said. I was worried. The man was about my Dad's age, but much bigger and stronger-looking.

On the day I left for college, I packed up the car. Sweater, tennis racquet, books. My first stereo system and box of records. Pretty soon the car was so full there was only room for Dad and me. We would drive together to New Hampshire. Mom would stay back home with the other kids.

I went to say good-bye to Mom.

"Bye," I managed, putting my arms around her. All of a sudden there was a lump in my throat.

"Bye," she replied. Her voice sounded funny, too. I was her firstborn child, and I was leaving home.

You notice that as I'm exploring each of these memories in my writing, I pay attention to the feelings connected to it: cozy, fearful, sad.

Exploring a memory includes looking into not only what happened but also how it affected you then, and how it affects you now. In her notebook, fourth grader Sara Mae Zerner remembers a close friend who moved away:

> In December my best friend, Conor, moved away. We did everything together. We made a treehouse and we found a secret pond. We called it the Homework Pond because we did our homework there. He moved to Atlanta, Georgia. I used to go swimming with him and go on little adventures.
> *I REALLY MISS HIM....*

Memories have a way of embedding themselves in special places. They soak into the rugs and sofas and walls and closets. If you want to recover a memory, try describing the place connected to it. Jennifer Young, a fifth grader, does this in the following notebook entry:

> ### Bye my Camp, I'll never forget you!!
>
> I'll never forget it. We actually sold our camp full of memories, love, fun, family. We had actually

sold our home away from home. There was no turning back. Our camp was no longer ours anymore. The word SOLD! was playing ping-pong in my head that whole day. Why did we have to sell it? That place is full of memories, that place is a memory, a memory that is now walking in our footsteps, just pushed away behind us. No more Katie, no more Megahn, no more Ben, no more concerts for the camp neighborhood, no more being stupid and riding a bike barefoot, no more taking boatrides in the shimmering sun, no more swimming in the cool, crisp water, and no more memories to write about, that is everything that went through my mind that day. I will never forget you my camp. You are truly a legend, a memory, and a friend in my life. I will never forget you.

These two writers have explored the range of feelings and images associated with losing a special friend or place. Of course, many of our memories are sunnier than that. This next notebook entry was written by Lauren Kurkowski, a sixth grader. I love its playful tenderness:

Shall We Dance, Daddy?

Every evening when my dad came home from work, before he could say but a mere hello I would blurt out that one and only famous line of mine: "Daddy, shall we dance?" I don't know why I bothered to ask after a while because the answer was always yes.

Daddy would lift me up and sing: "Shall we dance?" and he would dance me around the room.

What do you remember? What were you like when you were little? What reckless, stupid, funny things did you do? What stories do your relatives endlessly tell about you? What used to terrify you? Did you have a favorite stuffed animal? Blanket? Imaginary friend? Use your notebook to summon and capture the power of your past.

Many writers put into their notebooks other things besides words to help them remember. They do this as a way of preserving what they suspect they will later want to recall. What you put into your notebook is up to you, but here are some ideas of what you might include:

Drawings and doodlings. Lots of people prefer to express themselves through sketches or drawings. I've seen many notebooks that contain a mixture of written words and pictures.

Artifacts. One fourth-grade boy had a particular pen with which he wrote all his favorite stories. When it finally ran out of ink, he taped the inside of the pen into his notebook with the words: "*Here's my favorite pen. Date Died: 5/15/92.*" On another page, he taped balloon fragments from an unforgettable water balloon fight.

Fourth grader Sean McIlreavy has a page in his notebook entitled: THINGS I LOVE. He has clipped out photographs from magazines—of a rock musician, roller blades, a hockey stick, a fishing pole, baseball cards, a hundred-dollar bill—and taped them onto this notebook page.

The stuff I tape into my notebook includes tickets to sporting events I attended, autographs, and a backstage pass to a rock concert. Having these objects helps to keep me in touch with the actual experience. A few years ago, I received a letter from the poet Richard Margolis, author of *Secrets of a Small Brother*. This letter was important to me—I taped it into my notebook as well.

Articles. As you read the morning newspaper or flip through a magazine while waiting for your dental appointment, keep your eye out for any intriguing article that catches your eye. Often you can find an article or bit of news that could spark an idea for your writing.

When I find an article like that I clip it out and tape it into my notebook. The clippings in my notebook include matters of great personal significance (my grandfather's obituary), important world events (the day Nelson Mandela was freed from jail, the signing of the peace treaty in Bosnia), as well as more playful stuff:

- *Mayor forced to eat 12 pounds of bananas.*
- *Mating causes panda-monium: "Japan's two giant pandas mated twice at Tokyo's Ueno Zoo yesterday and the country settled back for a six-month wait to see if they will produce the first cub ever born in captivity outside China...."*

- **Fallen Object Investigated in Argentina:**
  *"A long, cylindrical object fell to earth May 6
  and disappeared in the dense jungle near
  the Argentine-Bolivian border, Argentine
  newspapers reported yesterday. There was
  no immediate confirmation from NASA. . . ."*

Any one of these articles might later be the catalyst for a story.

Photographs. My notebooks contain lots of photographs. Friends. My wife. My kids. The King of Tonga. My son's first school picture. Me.

I have one picture of me playing in the sand. I was just two or three at the time, sitting in a wooden boat that had no bottom. I see that picture and start thinking of all the younger Ralph Fletchers I left behind during my life. A photo like that can open up a whole almost-forgotten world.

See if you can get your hands on some pictures of you when you were younger. Some of the best photos to put into your notebook are the ones that make you uncomfortable—that silly expression you often have, the time you were on stage wearing a bunny costume, you sitting on the lap of your least favorite uncle. Photographs like that often spark the best writing.

Here's one tip: Leave space around whatever drawings, artifacts, clippings, or photos you put into your notebook. That way you have room to return to these objects and explore through writing what they mean to you, what memories they dredge up.

Using your notebook as a scrapbook can be fun. An artifact like a photograph contains powerful magic to bring a deeply buried memory to the surface of your mind. Most of us don't have photographs or videos of the most important memories of our lives. Don't worry. The mind itself has a gigantic storeroom of "mental photographs." All you need to do is to find a quiet place, close your eyes, and start browsing.

A few years ago I went to East Africa on a camera safari. At Serengeti National Park I saw giraffes, zebras, and lions all living in the wild. I saw flocks of flamingoes. I saw the snowy peak of Mt. Kilimanjaro rising above the grassy plain. During this trip I took lots of photographs, but I used my writer's notebook to record some of those things that were impossible to get on film.

Staying at camp something incredible *happened last night. It was dark, and I was walking from the building where dinner was being served back to my cabin. All of a sudden a man appeared. Without a word he put out his arm to stop me. For a few seconds, nothing happened. Then I saw them: wild elephants! I could feel the ground shaking as they moved through our camp in single file, moving fast in a kind of half-trot. I counted nine adult elephants, one behind the other. The last one was a baby elephant holding onto its mother's tail, straining to keep up with the others.*

Standing there, it had been much too dark to take a photograph. Later, with my knees still shaking, I went back to my camp and opened my notebook.

Someday elephants will appear in a poem or story of mine. But for now I'm more than happy to let them rumble through my notebook until I need them for anything else.

NINE

Writing that Scrapes the Heart

Shavonia Wynn is a fourth grader living in Columbus, Ohio. She wrote this passage in her notebook:

Growing Pains

When I was small, about five, I thought grown-ups were done with their crying years until one day we were looking for a house here in Columbus. Me and my sister were already in the van and my mom and dad came out and my mom accidentally closed the door on my brother's finger. All of a sudden my mom started crying . . . Then everything was settled down and I got in the backseat of the van. And I started crying not a loud cry, a *cry where you try to hold your tears back. I started crying not for my brother but for my mom! But I have never seen my dad cry—he probably does a secret cry like me. But anyway when my mom gets hurt I'm the first one at her side trying to comfort her because if she starts crying I cannot help crying myself. It scares me when a grown-up cries!*

Shavonia's writing doesn't fool around, doesn't try to be clever or smart or pretty. Intense writing like this holds nothing back. This chapter is about writing-as-lifejacket: the writing you do because your heart will burst if you don't write it.

You might think of writing in your notebook as being in your room with the door locked. Total privacy. You can wear whatever you want. Play whatever music you feel like playing. Read and think whatever you want. In this place you can be yourself. Or all the selves you want to be.

In this way the writer's notebook can work like a personal journal: a place to be completely honest with yourself. But being honest with yourself isn't easy. It takes practice to say exactly what you think and feel. And it takes courage—a willingness to face up to hard truths.

People often smile when they meet someone new. No matter how they're really feeling, they put on a pretend face that is calm, confident. That's fine, but in your notebook you don't have to pretend. In your notebook you can write honestly, even when things aren't going too well.

> *These days my life has no juice. No jazz. No bounce. No play. No dance. No parties. No friends visiting. All work and no play makes Ralph a dull boy. Since when did I get so boring? Whatever happened to the wide horizon I used to imagine I'd have as an adult? Whatever happened to just goofing around, having fun? Mom always said it's important to know what stuff makes you happy. She's right! I'm going to get a ticket to a Red Sox game. Better yet, I'm going to buy a new baseball glove, a new bat. Do some fishing. Maybe camp under the stars.*

Donna Barnes teaches fifth grade in North Berwick, Maine. She wanted each of her students to keep a writer's notebook, but she decided that if she was going to ask her students to keep one, she would have to keep one herself. In her note-book she wrote many personal entries, including this poem that she shared with her students:

Divorce

Divorce is like death
a partnership made and ended
sometimes abruptly
sometimes over decades

Divorce is a mystery story
to those involved
to those uninvolved

Divorce is a bomb
going off inside
the explosion of all you
once stood for
once believed in

Divorce for the kids
is a moment stood
still
it's a betrayal
it's the lie of their
lifetime

Divorce is the
symbol of failure
once and forever

In her notebook, Nicole Rogers began writing about her father:

My Dad

Why didn't my dad care about me? Why did he hurt me so much? How could he do this to me? These are questions that I probably will never know the answer to. Thinking about what my dad did to me makes my blood bubble like Hot Lava! He had no right to do that to me. I HATE HIM!!!
WHY??
Why did he "pretend" to be my friend?

Nicole is telling the truth about her life. After a few days, Nicole continued writing in her notebook with the same honest, emotional tone:

Well right now I am very clear minded. I don't know what to write about. I mean a lot of things have happened today but I just feel like things just happen and that's it. I don't like to talk about my feelings with anyone because it makes me cry sometimes, and I get embarrassed. I just don't feel very functional right now. I am tired. I cannot keep my head up or my eyes open for one more minute. I'm drifting off. No. No I've just got to got to got to SLEEP. . . . ZZZZZZZZZZZZZZZZ. "Huh?" No, I can't fall asleep. I'm too tired to go to sleep. I don't feel good. I want to go home.

I'm mad and my life is coming to an end. I feel like I don't have any friends anymore. Why was I brought into this world? I don't belong here. It wasn't MY CHOICE. I know that EVERYONE would be better off without me. IT'S TRUE! I'm nobody, everyone pretends to be my friend but are always writing notes about me like _____, _____, _____. There are even more people.

These words I cannot speak of, they can only be done in lead or ink and that's all I have to say.

Some writers use their notebooks to record *secrets*, things they don't want anyone to read, ever. I do. In this book I have shared entries from my notebook, but there are many things written there that are too personal to share with anyone. But those secrets are an important part of me. And they need to be in my notebook if it is going to reflect my interior life accurately.

Are there secrets, big or little, you might like to write about? Use a code if you're worried about someone reading your notebook and finding out. Writing about a secret doesn't always lead to a finished masterpiece, but it usually feels better, at least to me, putting the secret into words.

Some of my most important writing comes in the letters I write. Letters give me a way to express some important, difficult truth I want to tell someone. Here is a letter I wrote a few years ago to a friend who kept asking to borrow money.

Dear _____,

I'm writing about your request to borrow money. I heard that _____ sent you $150, so your immediate crisis is over. But you've got no job—I'm sure sooner or later you're going to run into other money problems. I've decided I'm

not going to lend/give you any more money. It's
hard to write this to you. I don't mean to be
hard-hearted. I worry about you a lot. It's just
become more and more clear to me that sending
you money only gets in the way of your solving
the problem because it makes you dependent on
me. In the long run I'm not the solution to
your problem. In the long run, you've got to
find a way to solve your job/money problems on
your own.

I'll give you any help I can—except cash—
to help you solve that problem. I mean that.
Give me a call if you want to think through job
stuff. Come over some weekend and I could help
you work on your resume . . .

Writing this letter was really hard. I taped a
copy of it into my writer's notebook because it just
might have been the single most important thing
I wrote that year.

You can use your writer's notebook to write a
letter to anyone, even if it is a letter you will not—
or cannot—send. (I know several young writers
who have written love letters to another boy or

girl, knowing full well that there is *NO WAY!* these letters will ever be sent.) Billy Kraus, a fourth grader, wrote the following letter in his notebook:

Dear Dad,

Why did you leave? You said that Mom asked you to leave, but she said you just left. Where are you right now? I'd send you this letter but I don't know where you are. I don't know whether to like you or not. I don't know who to believe. I don't trust anyone anymore. I thought you were good to us. But now I'm wondering. If Mom asked you to leave I know why. Because you never leave money in the bank. Right now was the worst time to leave.

from ????

P.S. Please write back.

While visiting a junior high English class, I mentioned to the students that it's possible to write a letter to anybody, even someone no longer alive. There was a boy in the class whose mother had committed suicide the previous year. He had never written about this tragedy, but now he took out his notebook and wrote a letter to her. The letter began:

Hi Mom.
It's me.

With these four words he broke the silence.

TEN

Writing that Inspires

The notebook can work as a scrapbook to collect important relics from your life. But you can also use your notebook as a different sort of scrapbook, a place to gather writing that inspires you. Often you read something that leaves you shaking your head in admiration. When that happens, stop and take note. Either copy it into your notebook, or clip and tape it in.

> *Acres of sunflowers brighten the land in the summer, their heads alert, expectant. By fall they droop like sad children, waiting patiently for the first snow and harvest.*
>
> KATHLEEN NORRIS, *Dakota: A Spiritual Geography*

His heart was slamming inside his chest like something that wanted out.

CORMAC MCCARTHY, *The Crossing*

Collecting writing like this isn't just an idle hobby of mine—I need these words the way a lion needs meat. I go back to reread them over and over again. Writing like this keeps me going when I start to falter. My truest inspiration comes from the poems and paragraphs of real people practicing the writing craft.

The first time I taped somebody else's writing into my writer's notebook I felt a little guilty. It seemed too easy, as if I was getting away with something. Today I have a different attitude. I've learned that if I am going to write well, I need to surround my words with the beautiful writing of others.

My friend Jim is a phenomenal basketball player. For years I've noticed a surprising thing— I seem to play better when I'm playing on the same team with Jim. Like most people, I tend to rise to the level of the competition I'm playing with.

That's why I collect memorable writing, and why I want to encourage you to sprinkle sparkling throughout your own notebook. Writing like this will help to raise the quality of what you write.

It's important for me to have this writing gathered together in one place. What kinds of writing do I collect in my notebook? I look for writing I admire, writing that haunts, dazzles, or surprises me in some way. I gather all sorts of stuff—sentences and paragraphs, poetry/fiction/nonfiction, work both published and unpublished, writing by adults as well as by children. For example, I taped in a poem my son, Adam Curtis, wrote in second grade:

The Moon

The moon is a jewel
racing through the night
with bare branches
like bony fingers
trying to grab it.
Why not?
Why not?

This untitled poem by Chase Whitmire, a New Hampshire fourth grader, also has its place in my writer's notebook:

> I am the person who
> Frantically plays with the leaves,
> Dances with the sun,
> Smiles at the moon,
> Follows the stars,
> Puts my arm around the wind's shoulder,
> Tells secrets with the water.
> And I think I'm special
> To have such adoring to do.

Sandra Cisneros is one of my favorite authors; on almost every page of her books, I find a phrase or sentence that leaves me shaking my head. Sometimes I copy an entire passage into my notebook; other times it's just a sentence. In her book *Woman Hollering Creek*, there is one story about a girl who likes a boy named Max Lucas Luna Luna. One afternoon she finds herself riding her bike through his neighborhood. The idea that she might run into this boy makes her jumpy. This is how Cisneros describes the feeling:

> *Just knowing Max Lucas Luna Luna might appear*
> *was enough to make my blood laugh.*

Paul Fleischman is a poet and novelist. In my notebook I have copied many bits of fine writing straight out of his powerful novel *The Borning Room:*

> *How I pitied mother and the others closed up in church like biscuits in the oven.*

> *(Description of grandfather after a stroke): One side of his face seemed to have collapsed, like a building brought down by artillery.*

You'll find first-rate writing in picture books as well as novels. Some readers turn their noses up at the idea of reading a picture book. Big mistake! There is a load of sparkling writing in picture books, though you may not notice it on first reading. Writers do a lot of rereading; you may have to reread to find the best stuff.

In *The Relatives Come*, a picture book by Cynthia Rylant, there are some great lines about how life changes around the house when a horde of relatives invades:

You'd have to go through at least four different hugs to get from the kitchen to the front room. Those relatives!

It was different going to sleep with all that new breathing in the house.

In Jane Yolen's *Owl Moon,* a boy and his father go into the snowy forest to get a glimpse of an owl. This book is full of gorgeous writing:

> The shadows
> were the blackest things
> I had ever seen.
> They stained the white snow.

Use your notebook as a container to hold all the beautiful writing you collect, all the words that make you sit up straight. You can also collect wise words about writing:

The secret wish of poetry is to stop time.

CHARLES SIMIC

The reasons for collecting sayings like this are purely selfish. Writing can be hard. You will want these words of encouragement nearby to help you through those days when the writing isn't going well.

Fiction is like a spider's web. It attaches itself ever so lightly (to the earth) but still it is attached at all four corners.

VIRGINIA WOOLF

The first draft is the down draft. You just get it down. The second draft is the up draft—you fix it up. The third draft is the dental draft, where you check every tooth, to see if it's loose or cramped or decayed, or . . . healthy.

ANNE LAMOTT, *Bird by Bird*

Many writers use their notebooks to gather very short sayings that really pack a wallop. These sayings are called aphorisms. Aphorisms can be thoughtful, inspirational, or just plain funny.

*You have two choices in life: you can dissolve into
the mainstream or you can be distinct. To be distinct, you must be different. To be different, you
must strive to be what no one else but you can be.*

ALAN ASHLEY-PITT

*Outside of a dog, books are man's best friend.
Inside of a dog, it's too dark to read.*

GROUCHO MARX

You may want to try something that many writers do—imitating the style of a piece of writing
you admire. This is called "writing off the text."
Your notebook is the ideal place to try an experiment like this. Not too long ago I stumbled onto
this poem by Valerie Worth:

seashell

My father's mother
Picked up the shell
And turned it about
In her hand that was
Crinkled, glossy and

114

Twined with veins,
The fingers rumpled
Into soft roses
At the knuckles, and
She said, "Why did
That little creature
Take so much trouble
To be beautiful?"

Whoa! This is my kind of poem—full of feeling, descriptive, simple yet profound. I love what the old woman says about the beautiful seashell, the way her words really seem to describe her own hands. I taped this poem onto a left-hand page in my notebook and left the other side blank, thinking that maybe later I would try to write a similar kind of poem of my own. A few months later, on that blank page, I wrote this:

Bulbs

My grandmother kneels
working the garden soil,
humming and half-smiling
as if making bread dough.

She's planting iris bulbs
knobby and almost as pale
as her own worn knuckles.
I watch her hands knead

the dark loaves of dirt
in that earthy confusion
of bulb and knuckle,
knuckle and bulb.

Stephanie Miller is a fifth-grade writer in North Berwick, Maine. She had read several books by Byrd Baylor, and was intrigued by the author's unusual style. In Byrd Baylor's books the text is arranged in short lines that look and sound very much like a poem. Stephanie read Baylor's picture book *Everybody Needs a Rock* and decided to write her own story in a style inspired by that book:

Everybody Needs a Father

Everybody needs
a father. Fatherless
children are always

trying to fight
their fears away.
You can't just
pick any father,
he has to be a
special one just
for you. I know
this girl in
Arizona that
picked the wrong
father and
ended up
running away
and never came
back. If you
don't know who to
pick lemme tell
you some rules
to getting just
the right father.

#1 It doesn't
matter what your
father looks like.
You gotta see

way into his soul
to pick the right
one. I know this
boy in Texas
who picked a
father because
he was handsome,
and his father
left him. Just left
without even saying
good-bye.

#2 You gotta pick
somebody who'll
spend time
with you.
Somebody who'll
go for walks
in the woods
with you and
take you on
trips. Trips that
take you
halfway across
California

but only
seem
like ten minutes 'cause
you're having such
a good time.

#3 Pick a father
who likes the sound
of little feet
around the
house and
doesn't mind
a fight with
your brother
once in a while.

Start gathering the writing you admire. You might have a special section in your writer's notebook for "Greatest Hits." Or you can do as I do and spread them out throughout your notebook. If you found any memorable writing in this book, you can use it to start your own All-Star writing team. Find writing that inspires you to grow into the kind of writer you hope to be.

ELEVEN

Rereading: Digging Out the Crystals

I am a rockhound. There's nothing sweeter than throwing a bunch of rockhounding gear (picks, shovels, sledges, goggles, bug spray, snake bite kit) into the car and heading off to a place like Herkimer, New York, to dig diamonds.

Not real diamonds. Herkimer is known for its lovely quartz diamonds (crystals that are "terminated," or pointed at both ends), which are stunning—even if they'll never make you rich. You find Herkimer diamonds in mineralized rock, and it takes hard work to get them: sometimes you have to dig down through a couple feet of dirt before you even reach the rock where the crystals lie.

Once you locate the rock you use a heavy tool like a crack hammer to carefully break off pieces of stone. On rare occasions, a piece of stone will crack away revealing a "gem pocket" filled with sparkling Herkimer diamonds. When these glittering bits come spilling out, you feel like shouting "EUREKA!" More often, you break off a chunk of rock that you suspect has crystals inside. You can haul the rock back to your car and bring it home. Later, in your basement or garage, you can leisurely work on the rock, crack it open, and find the crystals hidden inside.

A writer's notebook works in a similar way. If you get in the habit of paying attention to your world and writing down what you notice, your notebook will fill up with lots of intriguing stuff. Imagine your raw notebook material as mineralized rocks you have dragged home. In that rough stone all sorts of agates, crystals, and valuable fossils might be buried. It's up to you to dig them out.

How do you do that? How do you separate sparkling crystal from dull rock?

There is no simple answer to that question. But for most writers the answer begins with *rereading* all the stuff you've collected so you can sift out the most valuable pieces, bits that can spark your own original writing.

Rereading. It sounds easy, and in some ways it is. But reading your writer's notebook is different than reading a book. When I read a book or a poem, I am focusing on being the reader. When I read my own notebook my attention is split: I am half-reader and half-writer, all at the same time.

When you go back and reread your notebook, try to be the best possible reader in the world. Reread carefully. Pay close attention, your mind sitting up straight even if your body is lying on a couch. If you're like me, you'll probably talk to yourself while you reread. Here are some "writer's questions" you might ask yourself, questions that will help you focus on your reactions to the entries:

- *What seems interesting/intriguing to me? What stuff do I most deeply care about? What ideas keep tugging at me?*
- *What seems bold and original? Where are the places where it's not just "the same old thing"? Where does the writing seem fresh and new?*

Rereading your writer's notebook involves a kind of sifting or panning for gold. Many entries leave you cold. You reread them and say to yourself: "No . . . nope (Why did I put that in here?). . . . No way. . . . So what?" But every so often you find a notebook entry that makes you say: "Mmmm, you know, this is sort of interesting. . . ."

Reread carefully. And don't expect to find perfectly polished little gems all ready for publication because you probably won't. That almost never happens to me. Instead, look for potential, places where you suspect you might have something good if you develop and polish your words. It might be as little as one sentence that you find. While rereading my notebook, I recently came upon this sentence:

Morning twilight begins to erase the blackboard of stars.

Nice! This sentence had a certain ring when I first wrote it down. Now, months later, the idea of *erasing the blackboard of stars* still sounded fresh and new. I've always been fascinated by dawn and dusk, the most mysterious times of day, the cracks between the worlds of light and dark. I copied this sentence onto a blank page of my notebook and began to freewrite about the twilight, writing down whatever thoughts and images came into my head. This would eventually turn into a picture book, *Twilight Comes Twice.*

Reread. Look for seeds. Look for sparks.

Author Jackie French Koller thinks of her notebook as an "idea file" to spark her writing. One day she cut an article from the *Boston Globe* about a foster child looking for a permanent family. Much later, she came back to this article. She combined it with the memory from her childhood, growing up next to a family of foster children. This sparked the idea for her novel *A Place to Call Home.*

While rereading, you may dig up a scientific fact that rouses your imagination. The poet Lillian Morrison reread one of her old notebooks and found a fact about earthworms that she had copied out of a biology textbook: "Connective vessels in the esophagel region that are able to pulsate and pump are referred to as 'hearts.' The earthworm has five 'hearts' in the front part of its body."

This sounds exactly like textbook writing. But this bit of worm trivia amazed and intrigued her: a worm has not one but five hearts! Imagine how much fun Lillian Morrison had playing with this and similar worm facts in the following poem from *Whistling the Morning In:*

Oh, To Be an Earthworm

Oh, to be an earthworm.
It has five hearts.
When one is pained or pierced
the other four carry on.
It has no chin to "take it" on
no upper lip, no backbone
to keep stiff, just crawls
along in closest touch with the earth;
doesn't yearn at the stars
or stretch for the moon
but goes about its intimate
business, living its soft life
to the full, savoring it
inch by inch.

Remember that list of spider facts I've been collecting? One day while reading one of my notebooks, I was amazed at all the spider trivia I'd copied down. All at once, I felt an idea softly tugging at my sleeve, a story idea about a boy obsessed with spiders. The boy would keep his own kind of notebook, a "spider journal" that mixes facts about spiders and events from his own life. A few months later, I started working on a novel based on this idea, *The Spider Boy*.

Reread. Find a quiet place, and revisit the notebook entries you have written. Remember to pay close attention to what interests, excites, angers, or disturbs you. When you find something good—a dash of strong writing, the hint of a story idea, an ingenious idea for The Great American Novel—mark it in some way. Some writers circle or underline these parts of their writer's notebooks. When I find a promising entry, I often draw a big star in the margins with the note: *Poem Idea?* or *Story Idea?* or *Idea for Novel?*

Try to reread with a generous heart. Don't expect to find great polished writing. Remember: All you're looking for are a few writing ideas with potential. Something to build on.

On the other hand, don't take just any old thing. Try to be selective about what ideas you choose to develop. Trust your best ideas. See if you can find one or two ideas or entries that you could work into a piece of finished writing.

Leslie Davidson is a fourth-grade student in Dublin, Ohio. At the beginning of the year, Leslie shared a notebook entry with her fourth-grade classmates that began: *Winters and winters ago for Christmas we went to my aunt Kim's house. . . .*

Travis Kendall-Kerry, a classmate of Leslie's, loved that phrase *winters and winters ago.* Why? Who can say why a particular phrase or idea grabs any one of us? For some reason, this one struck a chord in Travis. He copied it into his own notebook and forgot about it. Nine months later, he reread his notebook and stumbled on to those words again: *winters and winters ago.* He pulled them out and used them in this poem about a special blanket he had as a child:

> it still lives packed up in boxes
> somewhere in the house
> that old blanket of mine
> you know
> i used to sleep with it
> winters and winters ago

Travis did exactly what professional writers do: He used his notebook to incubate a seed, in this case a seed he had found in someone else's writing. He left it for a time, reread his notebook in search of inspiration, and rediscovered this seed. When the time was right, the seed germinated quickly.

Ready for the bad news? The bald truth is that most of the stuff in your writer's notebook *never* germinates. A writer's notebook is filled with duds, dead ends, eggs that don't hatch, matches that fizzle out, rocks devoid of any crystals. When you first realize this, it's easy to get discouraged when you start to go back and reread your entries. If you're not careful, you can get into the habit of thinking: "There's *nothing* here—I can't use *any* of this stuff I wrote down. . . ."

"I don't get it," one fifth-grade girl said to me. "What's the point of putting stuff into your writer's notebook if you're never going to use it?"

"When I write an idea into the notebook I don't know whether or not I'll end up using it," I told her. "How can I tell which stuff I'll throw away, and which stuff I'll come back to? So I just write down everything and anything that grabs me. I figure that even if I get a few good ideas it's well worth it."

I told this girl something the writer Don Murray once wrote in one of his many books about writing: *Remember: It takes forty gallons of maple sap to make one gallon of maple syrup.*

This idea is with me every time I sit down to write. Maple sap is mostly water. To make syrup, you've got to boil off that water. Much of what you write in your writer's notebook is like that watery sap. There's no way around it: you have to boil off lots of water in order to make the syrup of your writing dark, thick, and sweet.

Thoughts about Notebooks
from Lillian Morrison

Lillian Morrison is a poet and anthologist who is best known for her collections of poems about sports. Her books include *The Sidewalk Racer, Whistling the Morning In, At the Crack of the Bat,* and *Slam Dunk.* She lives in New York City.

> *I have tons of notebooks into which I tend to throw everything—thoughts, ideas for books, early drafts of poems and letters, unfinished poems, dreams (including lines, phrases, or puns dreamed), passages from my reading that interest or move me, word lists, overheard bits of conversation, etc. Sometimes, when I need inspiration, I go back to an old notebook and a poem results. I always have a notebook next to my bed at night.*

TWELVE

Writing About Writing

Question: Do notebooks really represent the way to become a writer?

Answer: Nope. There is no single way to do that.

Question: But isn't it true that many writers consider their notebooks their most valuable tool?

Answer: Sure. But there are also writers who don't keep notebooks at all. Well-known children's book author Cynthia Rylant has never kept either a writer's journal, or notes for any writing. She says: "There's no unfinished manuscript to be found in my

desk. . . . I just don't write, and then I do,
and it's published."

Question: Oh. So where does that leave us?

Answer: Keeping a writer's notebook might
help you a great deal as a writer. It sure has
helped me, and it's been an invaluable
help for many writers I know. Keeping a
notebook might not be your thing, but you
probably won't know unless you try.

The best chance you have of making your
notebook work for you is to let it reflect your personal style. Do you like to cut out photos, articles,
strange headlines? If so, tape them into your notebook. Do you like to eavesdrop on conversations?
Jot them down. Do you make up dialogues in your
head? Write those down. Do you have strong reactions to the injustices of the world? Write down
your reactions—later you might be able to
develop them into essays. Are you a sports freak?
Tape a favorite basketball card into the first page
of your notebook. Do you collect odd words? Do
you find yourself coming up with ideas for poems
or stories? Write them down. Do you love to

doodle? Then make sure your notebook gives you ample space to doodle.

Your notebook should fit you the way a favorite pair of jeans fits your body. Let it reflect who you are. Every writer's notebook is a custom job; there is no one right way to keep one. Use it in a way that makes sense to you—even if I haven't described your kind of notebook in this book.

Writing opens doors in us we never knew existed. Writing helps us explore new worlds— inside and out. And it can be exciting to explore the world of writing. I have looked at dozens of writers' notebooks, and I have been struck by how many entries are about writing itself. Let me end this book with the words of some young writers on this subject:

> As I sit here the wind blowing on my face in Grandma's backyard I feel like a writer nobody to tell me what to write. No rules about writing as I sit here on the patio. I watch the squirrels running. My hand just wants to write and write.
>
> KILEY WILKERSON, fifth grade

When I was going through my "problem" (crying every night—not knowing why, and other things) I discovered a new "light" for myself. This light was writing. My teacher, Pastor Woody, my mom, and some other people think that it's great how I discovered writing as my way out. But I don't know why. Actually if I think about it I do, and it is great, but strange for me at the same time. I'm probably going to be a writer and psychologist (or I would like to be them) and it's GREAT!

REBECCA HAFNER, sixth grade

Notebooks are . . . well, it's like you have sparks from a campfire that could start a fire. They haven't yet, but they could any time.

MICHAEL CICCONE, first grade (!)

What Is a Lifebook?

A lifebook is something that you write all of your thoughts in. I personally like spiral notebooks.
    Before you purchase a lifebook there are a

few things you should do because if you don't you might have wasted some money.

1. *You should take a spiral notebook and a sewn notebook, open them to a page. Then, pretend you have a pencil in your hand. Which one feels more comfortable?*

2. *Pick the most comfortable one. Then take a big one and a little one. Use your pretend pencil again. Which one feels more comfortable now?*

3. *I like lines, but some people don't. Take the notebook you have now but get one with lines and one without. Get out your pretend pencil one more time, please. Which one is more comfortable?*

   Don't worry about how pretty it is. If that worries you, fancy it up at home. Personally I have a pretty dull notebook but I love it anyway. If you want, do step 4.

4. *Get a fancy notebook and a dull one. Get out*

your pretend pencil one last time. Which one feels more comfortable?

The notebook you pick should be your best friend. I hope you and your notebook have a happy life.

HEATHER PETRUZZI, fourth grade

I use my writer's notebook for ideas that pop into my head, or things I'm thinking about. My writer's notebook has very important things in it. I love my writer's notebook and I write in it EVERY CHANCE I GET. If I get writer's block, I can just look in my writer's notebook for ideas. I can use my writer's notebook now or 10 years from now, there's no telling when I can use it. My writer's notebook is my heart, my mind, and my soul.

ANNE RUBIN, fourth grade

The following six entries are from Besse Rawitsch, an eighth-grade writer from upstate New York:

The blank sheet of paper is the enemy and the pen the general of the army. It is up to me to conquer the unknown territory and win over the enemy.

When I pick up a pen it changes me. I'm not the same person. The way I talk, think, and everything changes. I feel more natural, more relaxed, and more like myself. That is a true power of the pen.

An author with a pen and sheet of paper but with no ideas is like a king with a crown and a throne but no kingdom. They can't do a thing.

Save every scrap you write. Whether it is good or not, it is worthwhile.

One of the reasons my writing is good is that I have bad communication skills. I can't confide in any one person. I trust no one. But I can let out all of my emotions through the pen. I can write out what I think and let everything out. Who is the paper going to tell? No one.

Writing is my escape. I write to free myself.

Finally, here are some thoughts from Briana Carlin, a fifth grader:

A notebook is where you keep dew drops from a dew drop morning. It's where the sun sets. It's the wind in your face at the beach looking out over the water. A notebook is where you're playing with your dog. It's where you have dreams about walking on rainbows. It's where the good feelings and the bad feelings spend the night.